Police Maths Test by Rian Crombie.

© 2018 by Rian Crombie. All rights reserved.

No part of this book may be reproduced in any written, electronic, recording, or photocopying without written permission of the publisher or author. The exception would be in the case of brief quotations embodied in the critical articles or reviews and pages where permission is specifically granted by the publisher or author.

Although every precaution has been taken to verify the accuracy of the information contained herein, the author and publisher assume no responsibility for any errors or omissions. No liability is assumed for damages that may result from the use of information contained within.

Visit the author's website at www.policemathstest.com.

First edition

ISBN: 9781980922223

Imprint: Independently published

THE TEST

The numerical reasoning test is designed to test your mathematical ability, ensuring that it is adequate to carry out the day to day duties of a Police Officer or PCSO. The test consists of 25 questions with multiple choice answers. The difficulty of the questions varies from challenging to fairly simple. Some questions need a good understanding of the area of maths which is being assessed, therefore it is important to thoroughly read through each question.

You will have 12 minutes to complete the 25 questions. The 12-minute limit is designed to add pressure, but remember to remain calm and work through each question logically, accurately and as quickly as possible. If you aim to spend approximately 30 seconds on each question, you should be able to finish nearly all the questions. You will not be allowed to use a calculator at any point in the test; however you will be given paper and a pen to work through the problems.

HOW TO PREPARE

The numerical reasoning test examines your mathematical skills and comprehension. As with any other test or exam it is important to thoroughly prepare; this involves learning or re-learning your basic maths skills. The tests in this guide will help you to brush-up on your skills so that you will eventually be able to pass the test with relative ease.
This, coupled with extensive revision and practice using internet and book resources, will help you become more confident and accurate in the test.

PRACTICE TEST 1

12 MINS

1. A garage is selling three used cars. The mileage on the first is 139,500, the mileage on the second is 120,500, and the mileage on the third is 160,000. What is the average mileage of the three used cars?

   A. 140,000
   B. 145,000
   C. 150,000
   D. 135,000
   E. 130,000

2. You are called to an accident 120 miles away. It takes you 1 hour 30 minutes to arrive at the accident site. What speed have you been driving at?

   A. 80
   B. 60
   C. 40
   D. 50
   E. 45

3. On a patrol around the local town you walk 10 miles. It takes you 2 hours. What speed do you walk at in miles per hour?

   A. 60 mph
   B. 20 mph
   C. 10 mph
   D. 5 mph
   E. 15 mph

4. During a traffic patrol you average 30 mph over 1 hour 20 minutes. What distance have you covered in this time?

   A. 32 miles
   B. 40 miles
   C. 50 miles
   D. 43 miles
   E. 45 miles

Page | 3

5. Sam, Steve and Mark are brothers. Sam is 36, Steve is 28 and Mark is 26. What is their average age?

   A. 29
   B. 32
   C. 31
   D. 33
   E. 30

6. There are four suspects in a police line up. Suspect A is 1.20m tall, suspect B is 1.25m tall, suspect C is 1.55m tall and suspect D is 1.6m tall. What is the average height of the suspects?

   A. 1.41m
   B. 1.40m
   C. 1.42m
   D. 1.39m
   E. 1.37m

7. The perimeter of the police dog training yard is 240 metres. The yard has a square perimeter. What is the average length of a side of the yard?

   A. 40 metres
   B. 50 metres
   C. 60 metres
   D. 120 metres
   E. 130 metres

8. The police are escorting approximately 540 football fans to the train station. A train can carry 135 people. How many trains will be needed to transport the fans?

   A. 2 to 3
   B. 4 to 5
   C. 6 to 7
   D. 8 to 9
   E. 9 to 10

9. Darren commutes to and from work every day from Monday to Friday. His office is 40 miles away from his house. How many miles does Darren drive per week?

   A. 200
   B. 400
   C. 800
   D. 1,000
   E. 1,200

10. John runs a marathon (26 miles) with 69 other runners. Every single runner completes the marathon. What is the combined distance run by all the runners?

    A. 1784
    B. 1830
    C. 1794
    D. 1820
    E. 1824

11. You bicycle for 2 hours at an average speed of 18 mph. What distance have you travelled in total?

    A. 9 miles
    B. 20 miles
    C. 36 miles
    D. 24 miles
    E. 22 miles

12. John is a tree surgeon who is paid to cut down a dead oak tree. The tree is 90 metres tall. John has to cut the tree into 4.5m sections. How many cuts will he have to make?

    A. 10
    B. 45
    C. 30
    D. 40
    E. 20

13. You own a market stall and sell 216 apples. You have sold apples to 36 customers. On average how many apples did each customer buy?

    A. 4
    B. 6
    C. 8
    D. 12
    E. 14

14. The Metropolitan Police have 1,200 police officers on duty. They want 300 areas patrolled. How many police officers should go on each patrol?

    A. 2
    B. 3
    C. 5
    D. 6
    E. 4

15. A leisure complex has three pools: pool A, pool B and pool C. What is the area of swimming pool A?

    A. 6 m²
    B. 10 m²
    C. 12 m²
    D. 14 m²
    E. 21 m²

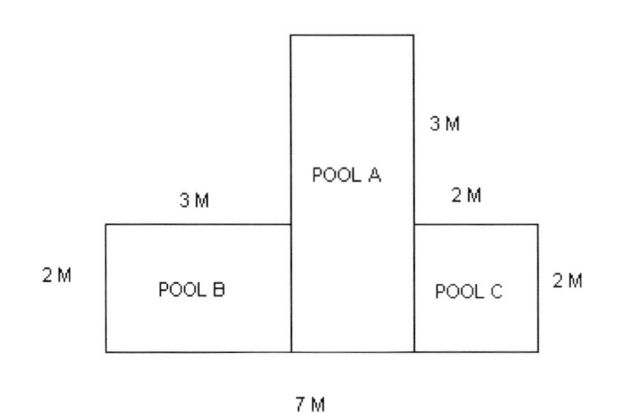

16. What is the average weekly wage of a team of five people whose individual wages are: £59.00, £61.00, £64.00, £76.00 and £80.00?

    A. £64
    B. £68
    C. £73
    D. £76
    E. £77

17. Response times to emergency calls vary throughout the week; on Monday it is 7 minutes, on Tuesday it's 7 minutes, on Wednesday it's 5 minutes, on Thursday it's 6 minutes, on Friday it's 9 minutes, on Saturday it's 8 minutes and finally on Sunday it's 7 minutes. What is the average response time?

    A. 6 minutes
    B. 5 minutes
    C. 8 minutes
    D. 9 minutes
    E. 7 minutes

18. There are 7 new PCSO's at a Wolverhampton police station. Their ages are 18, 19, 21, 24, 28, 29 and 36. What is their average age?

    A. 22 years old
    B. 24 years old
    C. 25 years old
    D. 26 years old
    E. 27 years old

19. There are 150 guests at a Spanish holiday complex. 50 of the guests are British, 35 are German, 10 are French, and 5 are Italian. The rest of the guests are Spanish. What percentage of guests are Spanish?

    A. 33.33%
    B. 32%
    C. 33%
    D. 66.66%
    E. 70%

20. Using the chart below, on average how many people would use the bus over a 4-month period?

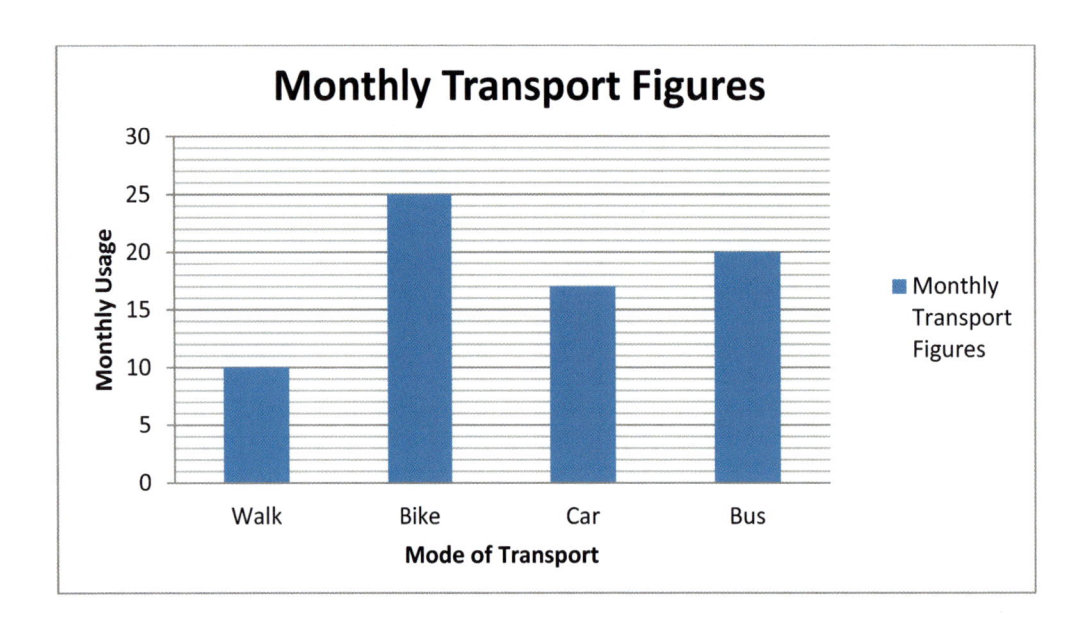

Monthly Transport Figures

A. 40
B. 45
C. 60
D. 80
E. 90

21. Using the chart above, calculate the combined total of people who walk and use a bike as a mode of transport per month?

A. 25
B. 30
C. 35
D. 40
E. 45

22. The police receive 1,200 applications for every 60 available posts. What is this as a fraction?

A. 4/1
B. 20/1
C. 30/1
D. 40/1
E. 45/1

23. A container ship carries 1,000 barrels. Each barrel contains 330 litres of oil. How much oil is contained in the barrels?

A. 330 litres
B. 3,300 litres
C. 33,000 litres
D. 330,000 litres
E. 3,300,000 litres

24. A bike company has 12 factories each producing 102 bikes a day. How many bikes does the company produce per day?

A. 1,004
B. 1,040
C. 1,204
D. 1,224
E. 1,226

25. A carpet factory operates 24 hours a day. If the factory produces 10 carpets an hour, how many carpets are produced in a day?

A. 220
B. 240
C. 260
D. 280
E. 290

PRACTICE TEST 2

12 MINS

1. In a biscuit tin there are 28 biscuits. If you were to divide these equally between a family of 4, how many biscuits would each family member get?

   A. 7
   B. 4
   C. 8
   D. 3.5
   E. 5

2. A plane can carry 180 passengers. There are 36 rows on the plane. How many passengers are there on each row?

   A. 9
   B. 6
   C. 7
   D. 8
   E. 5

3. You have been driving for 2 hours 15 minutes at a constant speed of 48 mph. How far have you driven so far?

   A. 180 miles
   B. 108 miles
   C. 104 miles
   D. 140 miles
   E. 144 miles

4. A sprinter runs 200 metres in 22 seconds. How long would it take him to run 2,000 metres if he continued to run at the same speed?

   A. 3 minutes 40 seconds
   B. 3 minutes 20 seconds
   C. 4 minutes 20 seconds
   D. 3 minutes 15 seconds
   E. 4 minutes 15 seconds

5. Samantha is a carpenter. She makes 3 oak tables for a family. The first table top measures 0.75 x 2 metres, the second measures 1.5 x 3 metres and the third measures 1.0 x 3 metres. What is the average area of the table tops?

A. 5 m²
B. 4 m²
C. 3 m²
D. 2 m²
E. 2.5 m²

6. Five students buy a pizza each. Each pizza costs £5.20. The students are each given 10% discount. What is the total bill for the students?

A. £23.20
B. £23.40
C. £23.60
D. £24.40
E. £24.60

7. At a campsite there are 240 tents. During a flood, 2.5% of the tents are damaged. How many tents were damaged during the flood?

A. 6
B. 8
C. 5
D. 9
E. 4

8. In your savings account there is £13,000. You decide to withdraw 40% to buy a car. How much money do you withdraw?

A. £520
B. £5,200
C. £7,200
D. £8,000
E. £8,200

9. You own a Ford Fiesta which is currently worth £8000. Since you bought the car it has depreciated in value by 30% of its original value. How much was the original value of the vehicle?

A. £8,240
B. £11,400
C. £10,400
D. £12,400
E. £12,450

10. A ticket for a football match costs £12. If 12,000 people go to the game, how much in total will ticket sales make?

A. £14,400
B. £144,000
C. £288,000
D. £144,0000
E. £420,000

11. A solicitor charges £28 per hour for legal services. If you hired a solicitor for 12 hours, how much would you be charged?

A. £326
B. £336
C. £374
D. £436
E. £442

12. At Uxbridge Grammar there are 200 students. 15 of the students get straight A's. What is this as a percentage?

A. 7.5%
B. 10%
C. 15%
D. 30%
E. 45%

13. You find a missing wallet in the street. It contains a £10 note, two £5 notes, three £1 coins, a 50p coin and six 2p coins. How much is in the wallet?

A. £22.72
B. £22.62
C. £24.62
D. £23.56
E. £23.62

14. Your car does 35 miles to the gallon. The car takes 8 gallons of petrol full. If you were to drive 560 miles how much petrol would you need?

A. 12 gallon
B. 14 gallons
C. 16 gallons
D. 18 gallons
E. 24 gallons

15. Two farmers, Jack and Tom, both own adjoining fields. What is the total combined area of both Jack's and Tom's fields?

A. 160m²
B. 240m²
C. 800m²
D. 1600m²
E. 2400m²

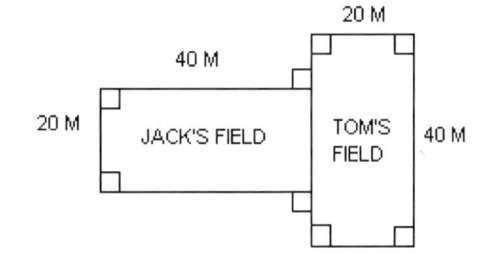

16. On average a bank repossesses 3 out of 150 homes every year. The village of Claxby has 1,000 homes. Under the above principle, how many homes would be repossessed in the village?

A. 10
B. 15
C. 20
D. 25
E. 30

17. A school has 15 classes with 23 students in each class. How many students are at the school?

A. 245
B. 325
C. 335
D. 445
E. 345

18. A restaurant serves 60 customers a night. If on average each customer spends £30, what is the total average for the night?

A. £180
B. £1,600
C. £2,400
D. £1,800
E. £1,260

19. A chocolate bar costs 59p. If you were to buy 6 chocolate bars, how much would it cost you?

A. £3.34
B. £3.45
C. £3.54
D. £4.24
E. £4.14

20. You fly a three-leg journey in a light aircraft. The total distance covered is 270 miles. What is the average distance of each leg?

A. 70 miles
B. 80 miles
C. 90 miles
D. 135 miles
E. 140 miles

21. A team of 12 explorers find the wreck of a ship. The ship contains 6 gold bars each worth £120,000. How much money does each team member make?

A. £40,000
B. £60,000
C. £100,000
D. £120,000
E. £130,000

22. Below is a pie-chart representing crime in the town of Upton. Based on an estimated 100 crimes, use the pie-chart below to estimate the number of burglary-related crimes.

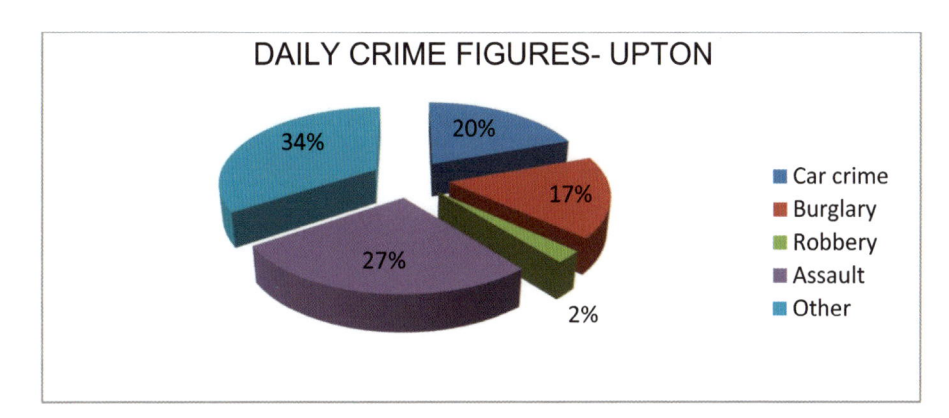

DAILY CRIME FIGURES- UPTON

- Car crime: 20%
- Burglary: 17%
- Robbery: 2%
- Assault: 27%
- Other: 34%

A. 17
B. 20
C. 27
D. 34
E. 170

23. A magazine on average contains 110 pages. If you bought seven magazines, how many pages are there in total?

A. 700
B. 720
C. 740
D. 770
E. 780

24. A car is travelling at 72 miles per hour. How many miles will it have travelled in 45 minutes?

A. 54
B. 52
C. 50
D. 48
E. 46

25. If carpet costs 1.20 per metre, how much will 35 metres of carpet cost?

A. £45.00
B. £43.75
C. £44.00
D. £46.75
E. £42.00

PRACTICE TEST 3

12 MINS

1. If 70% of £500 has been spent, how much money remains?

   A. £125
   B. £130
   C. £140
   D. £150
   E. £160

2. A multi-storey office has 7 floors, and each floor has 49 employees. How many members of staff work in the multi-storey office?

   A. 257
   B. 343
   C. 357
   D. 423
   E. 475

3. Following some road works on the M1 the highways agency need their 5 vehicles to collect 1,250 cones. On average how many cones do each of the 5 vehicles have to collect?

   A. 125
   B. 200
   C. 250
   D. 500
   E. 525

4. Laura buys three items: a pair of shoes, a dress, and a coat. The items totalled £340. If the shoes were £59.99 and the coat was £139.99, how much was the dress?

   A. £138.02
   B. £138.00
   C. £140.02
   D. £142.00
   E. £144.00

5. At Telford school there are 200 school students. 25 students get straight A's. What is this as a percentage?

A. 12.5%
B. 10%
C. 15%
D. 30%
E. 25%

6. A carton of milk costs £1.19. How much change would you have left from £5.00 if you bought one carton?

A. £2.81
B. £3.61
C. £3.71
D. £3.81
E. £4.05

7. You are driving down a motorway at 108 mph. How far do you travel in 25 minutes?

A. 47 miles
B. 45 miles
C. 44 miles
D. 42 miles
E. 41 miles

8. A fast jet is flying at a speed of 270 mph. The distance from airfield A to airfield B is 90 miles. How long does it take to fly from A to B?

A. 20 minutes
B. 24 minutes
C. 22 minutes
D. 26 minutes
E. 28 minutes

9. You are travelling down a motorway. Your journey has lasted 50 minutes and you have covered 125 miles. What speed have you been travelling at?

A. 162 mph
B. 155 mph
C. 160 mph
D. 152 mph
E. 150 mph

10. The police on average respond to 25 emergency calls a day. How many do they respond to in a week?

A. 160
B. 165
C. 170
D. 175
E. 180

11. Lincolnshire, Yorkshire and Lancashire all have new police helicopters. It takes the Lincolnshire helicopter 15 minutes to fly to Leeds, the Lancashire helicopter takes 35 minutes and the Yorkshire helicopter takes 10 minutes. What is the average time it takes these three helicopters to get to Leeds?

A. 15 minutes
B. 20 minutes
C. 25 minutes
D. 30 minutes
E. 35 minutes

12. A car park has 500 available spaces. On a busy day 75% of these are full. How many full car parking spaces are there on a busy day?

A. 375
B. 350
C. 325
D. 320
E. 310

13. You have £50 in your wallet and spend 70% of it on shopping. How much money have you spent on shopping?

A. £30
B. £35
C. £40
D. £50
E. £45

14. The Metropolitan police force has 120,000 officers. 3% of these officers are due to retire. How many officers will retire?

A. 360,000
B. 36,000
C. 360
D. 36
E. 3,600

15. The road tax for your car cost £120 in 2007. In 2008 it increases by 10%. How much is the road tax in 2008?

A. £121.20
B. £132
C. £142
D. £152
E. £152.20

16. A school decides to buy 12 laptops costing £850 each. What is the combined cost for the 12 laptops?

A. £10,200
B. £10,400
C. £10,500
D. £10,600
E. £10,800

17. A metre of wool costs 62p. How much would it cost to buy 6 metres of wool?

A. £3.72
B. £3.62
C. £3.82
D. £4.72
E. £5.12

18. Sally is riding her horse in a cross country competition. She has been told that she has to complete the course in 2 hours and 30 minutes. If divided into equal quarters, how long should she aim to spend completing each phase?

A. 35 minutes
B. 37.5 minutes
C. 35.5 minutes
D. 38.5 minutes
E. 39.5 minutes

19. There are 18 teams entered in a rugby competition. If there are 6 changing rooms, how many teams use each changing room?

A. 2
B. 4
C. 6
D. 3
E. 5

20. Using the diagram below, calculate the perimeter of the inner rectangle?

A. 16.4 cm
B. 17.2 cm
C. 17.8 cm
D. 18.4 cm
E. 18.8 cm

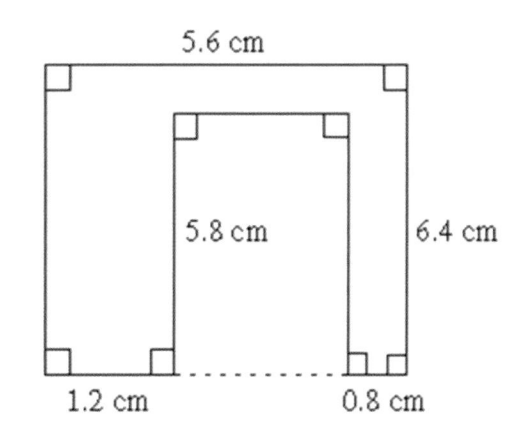

21. A room measures 20m by 5m. If I wanted to carpet 50% of it and I had 60 square metres of carpet available, how many square metres would I have left after finishing the task?

   A. 5m²
   B. 10m²
   C. 15m²
   D. 20m²
   E. 25m²

22. If a ferry journey of 490 miles takes 7 hours, what is the average speed of the ferry?

   A. 55 mph
   B. 60 mph
   C. 65 mph
   D. 70 mph
   E. 80 mph

23. A multi-storey car park has 8 levels. Each level has 111 car parking spaces. How many cars will be in the car park when it is full?

   A. 784
   B. 888
   C. 988
   D. 8,888
   E. 9,988

24. The office sweepstake wins £1,500. If this is divided by 25 employees, how much does each employee win?

   A. £30
   B. £40
   C. £60
   D. £80
   E. £85

25. Below is a line graph showing car sales for Manby Autos from January to April. Calculate the total combined car sales for February and March.

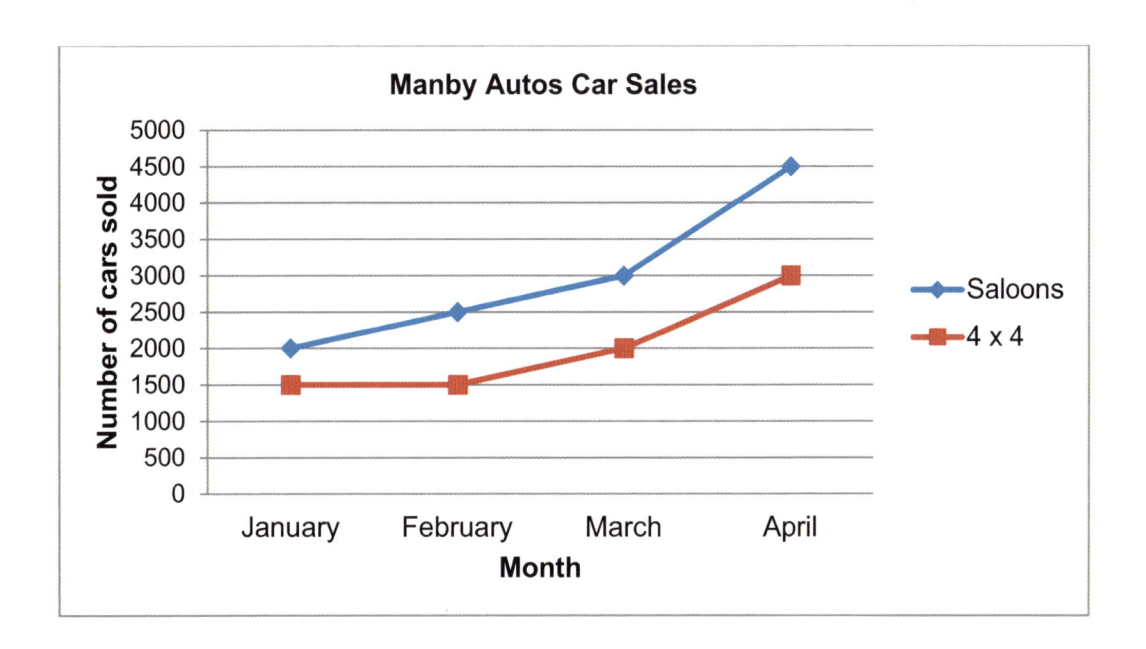

Manby Autos Car Sales

A. 900
B. 8,000
C. 9,000
D. 10,000
E. 12,000

PRACTICE TEST 4

12 MINS

1. A yearly golf subscription costs £150 in 2007. It is expected to rise by 15% in 2008. How much will the yearly subscription cost in 2008?

    A. £172.50
    B. £172.20
    C. £172
    D. £165.72
    E. £162.50

2. In a cross country competition there are 138 runners, 23 runners do not finish the race. What is this as a fraction?

    A. 1/5
    B. 1/6
    C. 1/8
    D. 1/12
    E. 1/4

3. A football pitch is approximately 110 metres long. If you had 11 football pitches, one after the other, how long would the total distance be?

    A. 1,110 metres
    B. 1,420 metres
    C. 1,390 metres
    D. 1,440 metres
    E. 1,210 metres

4. One out of twelve people in a group of football fans support Manchester United. If there are 2880 football fans, how many <u>do not</u> support Manchester United?

    A. 2420
    B. 2640
    C. 2680
    D. 2740
    E. 2520

5. A constable leaves the house at 08.00 hours and returns at 14.45 hours. How many hours has he been away from home?

A. 5 hours 50 minutes
B. 5 hours 45 minutes
C. 6 hours 50 minutes
D. 6 hours 45 minutes
E. 6 hours 15 minutes

6. You go to your local supermarket. You decide to buy some tomato soup. Each tin costs 14p. How much will 6 tins cost in total?

A. 60p
B. 64p
C. 70p
D. 84p
E. 86p

7. One carpet tile measures 5cm by 5cm. How many tiles are required to cover a floor which measures 10m by 2m?

A. 70
B. 75
C. 80
D. 85
E. 90

8. One power station supplies power to 34,000 homes. How many homes would 4 power stations supply?

A. 126,000
B. 128,000
C. 138,000
D. 148,000
E. 136,000

9. A drum contains 23 litres of oil. If a ship carries 11 drums of oil onboard, how many litres of oil are there altogether?

A. 233 litres
B. 241 litres
C. 253 litres
D. 263 litres
E. 266 litres

10. A football match has an average of 32,000 spectators. There are 26 football matches a year. What is the total number of spectators throughout the year?

A. 83,200
B. 832,000
C. 964,000
D. 110,600
E. 124,000

11. A library has 25 shelves of books. Each shelf holds 700 books. How many books are in the library?

A. 1,750
B. 17,050
C. 17,500
D. 35,000
E. 38,500

12. At an allotment there are 3 plots: plot A, plot B and plot C. Using the diagram below, calculate the area of plot B.

A. 1,000 m²
B. 2,500 m²
C. 2,000 m²
D. 3,000 m²
E. 100 m²

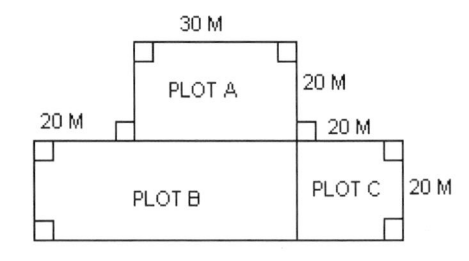

13. What is the average value of the following: 14, 28, 47, 47, 60 and 104?

A. 50
B. 53
C. 55
D. 60
E. 62

14. There are 44 police forces in the United Kingdom. Each police force has 14 Senior Officers. How many Senior Officers are there in total?

A. 561
B. 606
C. 616
D. 861
E. 882

15. A company has to dismiss 1 out of 6 of their employees. If the company employs 636 people, how many will the company have to dismiss?

A. 96
B. 103
C. 106
D. 126
E. 132

16. If 6 out of 24 police officers become traffic officers, what is this as a fraction?

A. 1/4
B. 2/4
C. 1/8
D. 1/6
E. 1/3

17. You go to the local shop and buy a magazine costing £2.40 and a drink costing £1.12. How much change do you get from a £10 note?

A. £6.52
B. £4.48
C. £5.52
D. £6.48
E. £6.56

18. A cruise ship can carry 90,000 passengers. On this occasion the ship is only 75% full. How many passengers are on board?

A. 6,750
B. 13,500
C. 54,500
D. 67,500
E. 68,250

19. A car garage sells 50 cars per month. 2 % of these are returned with engine problems. How many cars with engine problems are returned to the car garage each year?

A. 6
B. 9
C. 13
D. 15
E. 12

20. A Formula 1 car drives 660 miles in 3 hours 40 minutes. What is its average speed?

A. 160 mph
B. 190 mph
C. 180 mph
D. 185 mph
E. 190 mph

21. You can run 2 miles in 18 minutes. How long does it take you to run 0.5 miles at this speed?

A. 4 minutes 30 seconds
B. 5 minutes
C. 6 minute 30 seconds
D. 4 minutes 20 seconds
E. 5 minutes 10 seconds

22. You walk to school and it takes you 20 minutes. You know that you walk an average of 3 mph. How far is school from your house?

A. 2 miles
B. 1 mile
C. 6 miles
D. 4 miles
E. 5 miles

23. A farmer has 650 sheep. He keeps his sheep in 5 large fields. How many sheep does he have in each field?

A. 120
B. 130
C. 150
D. 160
E. 170

24. A delivery driver has to drive on average 12,000 miles a month. If the driver works every day in April, how many miles does he have to drive each day?

A. 200 miles
B. 300 miles
C. 350 miles
D. 387 miles
E. 400 miles

25. You withdraw 30% of your savings from an account which holds £600. How much remains in the account?

A. £360
B. £390
C. £420
D. £430
E. £450

PRACTICE TEST 5

12 MINS

1. A cruise ship has 13 rows of windows. If each row has 39 windows, how many windows are there in total?

   A. 498
   B. 507
   C. 527
   D. 618
   E. 627

2. In a car park there are 325 cars, and each car has 4 tyres and 1 spare tyre. How many tyres are there throughout the car park?

   A. 1,525
   B. 1,575
   C. 1,650
   D. 1,675
   E. 1,625

3. A greengrocer has a box of 360 strawberries. The greengrocer wants to make up punnets of strawberries, each with 36 strawberries in it. How many punnets of strawberries can the greengrocer make?

   A. 6
   B. 10
   C. 12
   D. 26
   E. 36

4. A ball of wool measures 3.3 metres. If you have 100 balls of wool, how many metres will there be?

   A. 3.30 metres
   B. 33.0 metres
   C. 330 metres
   D. 3,300 metres
   E. 660 metres

5. How many pieces of string measuring 1.25 metres in length can be cut from a ball which is 100m long?

A. 12.5
B. 125
C. 80
D. 250
E. 250

6. One case containing 42 cartons of orange juice costs £6.30. How much will two cartons of orange juice cost?

A. 10p
B. 15p
C. 25p
D. 30p
E. 45p

7. A moped is travelling at a speed of 35 mph. How long does it take to travel 7 miles?

A. 6 minutes
B. 10 minutes
C. 24 minutes
D. 8 minutes
E. 12 minutes

8. A train travels a total distance of 540 miles at a constant speed of 90 mph. How long does the journey last?

A. 360 minutes
B. 320 minutes
C. 240 minutes
D. 300 minutes
E. 280 minutes

9. What speed do you need to travel to go 100 miles in 2 hours?

A. 25 mph
B. 200 mph
C. 10 mph
D. 20 mph
E. 50 mph

10. A prisoner has escaped from prison. The prison is 20 miles away. You need to get there in 15 minutes. How fast do you need to drive?

A. 40 mph
B. 60 mph
C. 80 mph
D. 85 mph
E. 90 mph

11. A CD album has 49 minutes worth of songs. If each song is 3 minutes 30 seconds long, how many songs are on the album?

A. 7
B. 14
C. 15
D. 28
E. 18

12. A coach driver is making a journey form Land's End to John O'Groats. This is a distance of 420 miles. He has to make 7 equal stops. How many miles apart does each stop have to be?

A. 60
B. 80
C. 45
D. 70
E. 50

13. A train has 6 trams and each tram holds 80 tonnes of freight. What is the total weight of freight carried by the train?

   A. 380 tonnes
   B. 420 tonnes
   C. 480 tonnes
   D. 570 tonnes
   E. 580 tonnes

14. An office has 333 computer desks. If only 2/3 are used, how many are un-used?

   A. 33
   B. 90
   C. 111
   D. 222
   E. 22

15. Mike cycles every day for 30 minutes. How much time does he spend cycling over 8 days?

   A. 3.5 hours
   B. 4 hours
   C. 4.5 hours
   D. 5 hours
   E. 5.5 hours

16. A rugby club raises its annual subscription of £300 by 25%. What will the new subscription be?

   A. £345
   B. £360
   C. £370
   D. £375
   E. £385

17. A cinema ticket costs £5.00. If a pensioner is given a 15% discount, how much change will they get from a £20 note?

    A. £15.25
    B. £15.45
    C. £15.75
    D. £16.25
    E. £16.30

18. A circle has a diametre of 240 mm. What is the length, in centimetres, of the radius?

    A. 12 cm
    B. 18 cm
    C. 22 cm
    D. 6 cm
    E. 24 cm

19. Below is a bar chart showing yearly vegetable sales for a market in Castleton. What is the average yearly sale of mushrooms over the three years?

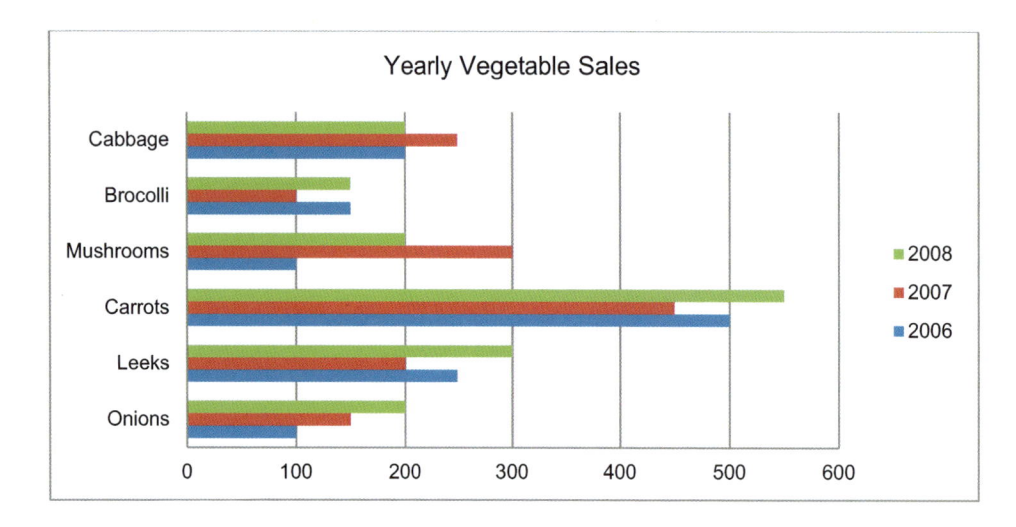

    A. 200
    B. 225
    C. 250
    D. 300
    E. 350

20. Roger needs to lay new turf in his garden. The whole of the garden will need new turf. Calculate the area of the garden that will need new turf.

    A. 66 ft²
    B. 112 ft²
    C. 128 ft²
    D. 132 ft²
    E. 144 ft²

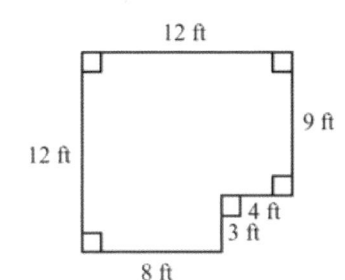

21. If I have £40 in my wallet and spend £13.75 of it, how much will I have left?

    A. £25.75
    B. £26.25
    C. £27.50
    D. £28.15
    E. £29.60

22. A motorist is travelling at 80mph. How far will he have travelled in 15 minutes?

    A. 10 miles
    B. 15 miles
    C. 12 miles
    D. 25 miles
    E. 20 miles

23. A prison cell holds two people. There are two prison areas: high risk and low risk. The high risk area has 123 cells and the low risk area has 334 cells. How many prisoners are there in the prison?

    A. 897
    B. 910
    C. 914
    D. 1,010
    E. 1,028

24. A food processing company has 10 people a week absent due to illness. How many people are absent due to illness in a year?

A. 520
B. 730
C. 1,040
D. 3,640
E. 3,650

25. Balmoray Police operate a three-shift working pattern in each day. Each shift has to have 22 police officers on duty. How many officers are required for a days work?

A. 66
B. 62
C. 60
D. 86
E. 132

PRACTICE TEST 6

12 MINS

1. In the Johnson family there are 7 people; 3 of them are female. What is this as a fraction?

   A. 2/3
   B. 4/6
   C. 3/7
   D. 6/15
   E. 1/3

2. You are at a traffic collision where a vehicle has crashed into a play area. As part of your documentation you need to calculate the area of the playing field. Using the diagram below, work out the area of the playing field and select the appropriate answer.

   A. 700 m²
   B. 900 m²
   C. 1,200 m²
   D. 1,300 m²
   E. 1,400 m²

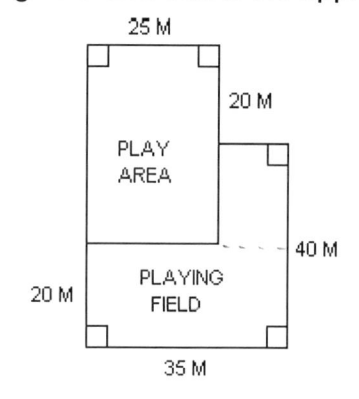

3. Your yearly salary is £40,000. You also receive a yearly bonus which is 15% of your salary. How much do you earn per year?

   A. £40,060
   B. £40,600
   C. £46,000
   D. £49,000
   E. £56,000

4. On a housing estate there are 34,000 homes. Of these homes 63% are semi-detached, 30% are detached, and the remainder are terraced houses. How many houses are terraced?

A. 23.8
B. 238
C. 2,380
D. 2,680
E. 23,800

5. You have two foot patrols a day. The total distance walked is 20 miles. If you walked an average speed of 4 mph, how long is each patrol?

A. 5 hours
B. 3 hours 30 minutes
C. 4 hours
D. 2 hours 30 minutes
E. 4 hours 20 minutes

6. You are tasked to drive your boss to a meeting 100 miles away. You will be driving at 60 mph. If you set off at 10:20pm, what time would you arrive?

A. 11:40pm
B. 12:00pm
C. 12:40pm
D. 12:20pm
E. 12:30pm

7. A criminal sprints at a speed of 10 metres every 2 seconds (10m/ 2 seconds). How long does it take him to run 1,000 metres if he continues at the same speed?

A. 100 seconds
B. 10 seconds
C. 200 seconds
D. 20 seconds
E. 25 seconds

8. You are at a fruit and vegetable stall at a market. If one apple costs 41p, how much would it cost to buy 11 apples?

A. £4.41
B. £4.21
C. £4.61
D. £4.67
E. £4.51

9. A car garage orders four new sport cars costing £41,000 each. How much in total has the garage spent on the new sports cars?

A. £124,000
B. £154,000
C. £164,000
D. £166,000
E. £168,000

10. A water tank has a maximum capacity of 200 litres. If the tank is 80% full how many more litres are required to fill it to its maximum?

A. 25 litres
B. 40 litres
C. 50 litres
D. 55 litres
E. 60 litres

11. If I spend £1.60, £2.35, £3.55 and £4.75 on a selection of goods, how much will I have spent in total?

A. £10.65
B. £11.60
C. £11.55
D. £12.25
E. £12.5

12. Below is a chart showing snowfall across the Lincolnshire region in 2004 in centimetres. What is the combined snowfall for January and May?

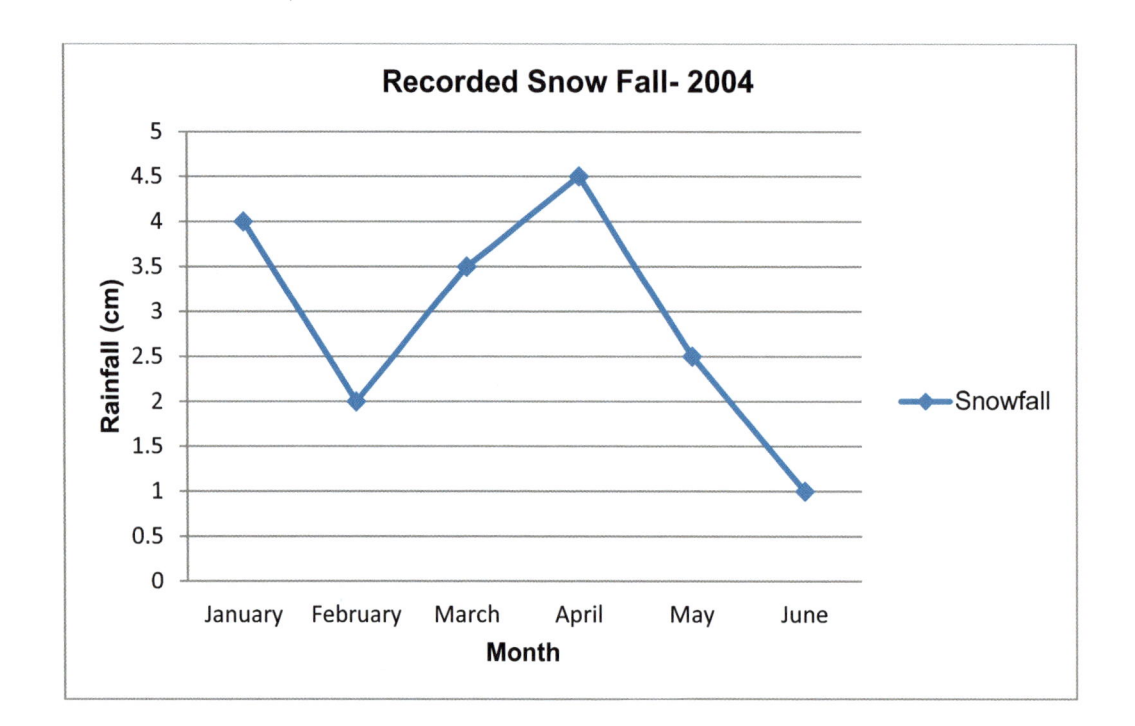

Recorded Snow Fall- 2004

(chart showing snowfall by month: January 4, February 2, March 3.5, April 4.5, May 2.5, June 1)

A. 5.5 cm
B. 6.0 cm
C. 6.5 cm
D. 7.0 cm
E. 8.5 cm

13. On Monday it takes Lucy 52 minutes to get to work. On Tuesday it takes 40 minutes, Wednesday takes 51 minutes, on Thursday it takes 1 hour 2 minutes and on Friday it takes 1 hour 30 minutes. How long did her average commute take?

A. 58 minutes
B. 62 minutes
C. 60 minutes
D. 61 minutes
E. 59 minutes

14. Paul is a 100 metre sprinter. During a weekend-long competition he runs the distance in 11 seconds, 9 seconds, 9.5 seconds and 11.5 seconds. What is the average time that Paul runs 100 metres in?

A. 9 seconds
B. 10 seconds
C. 11 seconds
D. 10.25 seconds
E. 10.5 seconds

15. One in fourteen people become a victim of car crime each year. In Saxby there are 224 people. On that basis, how many people per year experience car crime in Saxby?

A. 14
B. 16
C. 18
D. 20
E. 22

16. Lisa's weekly newspaper bill is £5.50 and the delivery charge is 35p per week. How much does she have to pay over six weeks?

A. £28.10
B. £31.10
C. £35.10
D. £35.20
E. £36.10

17. A gardener wants to gravel over the area shown below. One bag of gravel will cover 20 m². How many bags are needed to cover the entire garden?

A. 40
B. 55
C. 65
D. 75
E. 130

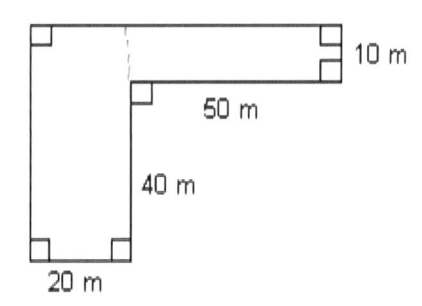

10 m
50 m
40 m
20 m

18. The gardener decides he is only going to gravel 20% of the garden. Using the above diagram, how many square metres will he be gravelling?

A. 26 m²
B. 300 m²
C. 130 m²
D. 240 m²
E. 260 m²

19. You stop and search 40 people, and 8 of them are arrested for possession of a class A drug. What is this as a fraction?

A. 1/3
B. 1/4
C. 1/6
D. 1/10
E. 1/5

20. There are 144 people entered into a raffle, 12 people each win a prize. What is this as a fraction?

A. 1/6
B. 1/8
C. 1/12
D. 1/24
E. 1/10

21. At a music festival there are 35,000 festival goers, 5% of these are under 16 years of age. How many festival goers were under 16?

A. 1500
B. 1750
C. 2500
D. 3500
E. 7000

22. At Christmas you buy 30 presents; 12 are bought for your family and 18 for your friends. What percentage was bought for your friends?

   A. 20%
   B. 30%
   C. 40%
   D. 60%
   E. 75%

23. Over one year, PC Smith files details of 600 drink driving cases. These are divided into 5 piles dependant upon how over the limit the drink driver was. If the piles are all equal sizes, how many are in each pile?

   A. 115 files
   B. 120 files
   C. 125 files
   D. 130 files
   E. 135 files

24. On average 1 out of every 30 people experience back problems in their lifetime. Out of 900 people, how many will experience back problems?

   A. 20
   B. 30
   C. 60
   D. 90
   E. 120

25. Below are a toy company's monthly sale figures. Calculate the average toy sales per month for the year.

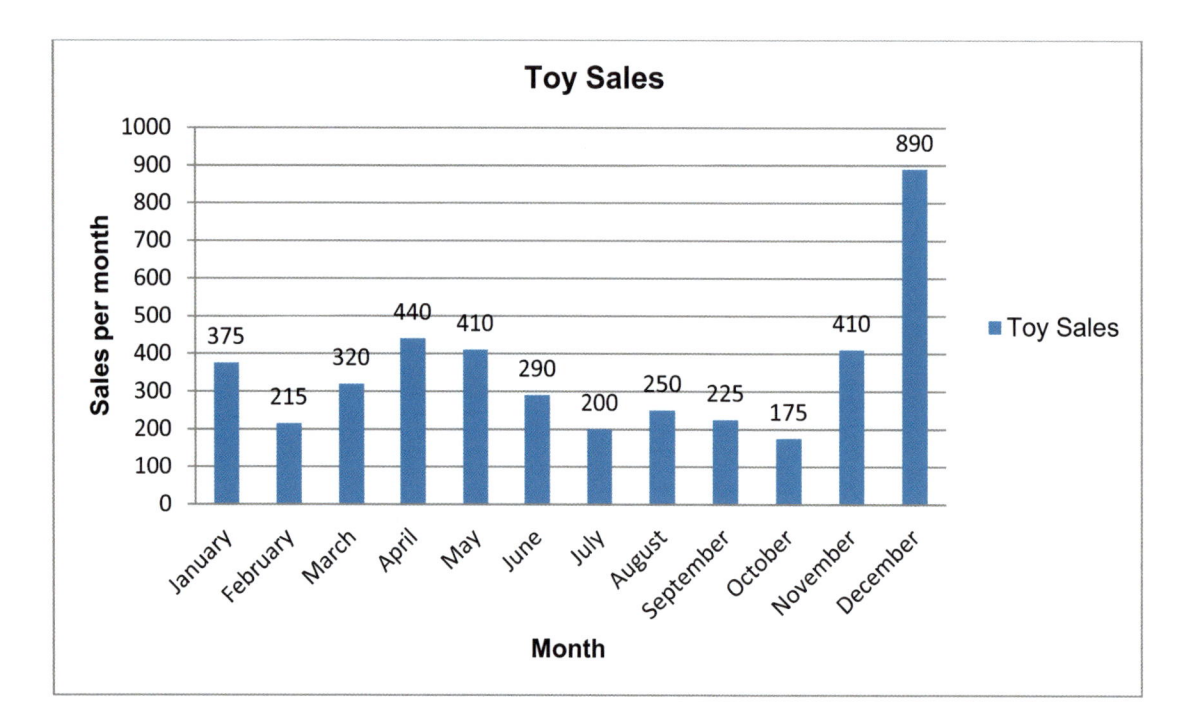

Toy Sales

Month	Sales
January	375
February	215
March	320
April	440
May	410
June	290
July	200
August	250
September	225
October	175
November	410
December	890

A. 350
B. 375
C. 450
D. 500
E. 700

PRACTICE TEST 7

12 MINS

1. Billy can run 1.5 miles in 12 minutes. How long does it take him to run 12 miles if he continues at the same speed?

   A. 1 hour 26 minutes
   B. 1 hour 12 minutes
   C. 1 hour 36 minutes
   D. 1 hour 6 minutes
   E. 1 hour 20 minutes

2. Jennifer runs 39 miles in 4 hours 20 minutes. What was her average speed?

   A. 12 mph
   B. 10 mph
   C. 9 mph
   D. 7 mph
   E. 8 mph

3. A helicopter flies a distance of 840 miles in 6 hours. What speed is it flying at in miles per hour?

   A. 140 mph
   B. 160 mph
   C. 150 mph
   D. 145 mph
   E. 135 mph

4. Emma works 5 days a week. Everyday she drives 20 miles to work, and 20 miles back. She drives at an average speed of 30 mph. How much time does Emma spend driving to work and back each working week?

   A. 6 hours 40 minutes
   B. 6 hours 15 minutes
   C. 6 hours 20 minutes
   D. 6 hours 45 minutes
   E. 7 hours

5. You are driving to an incident at 96 mph. The incident is 24 miles away. How long will it take you to get to the incident?

A. 12 minutes
B. 15 minutes
C. 10 minutes
D. 20 minutes
E. 25 minutes

6. You are driving at 42 mph for 20 minutes. How far have you come?

A. 14 miles
B. 20 miles
C. 17 miles
D. 15 miles
E. 16 miles

7. In a year 20,600 people are arrested. One quarter of these are over 50 years of age. How many people over 50 years of age are arrested?

A. 4,150
B. 4,300
C. 5,350
D. 5,200
E. 5,150

8. If 2 out of 10 entrants won at a dog show, how many would win if there were 100 entrants at the show?

A. 10
B. 15
C. 20
D. 35
E. 40

9. The pie chart below shows the percentage of aircraft sales across the world. If 10,000 aircraft were sold in total, how many were sold in the UK?

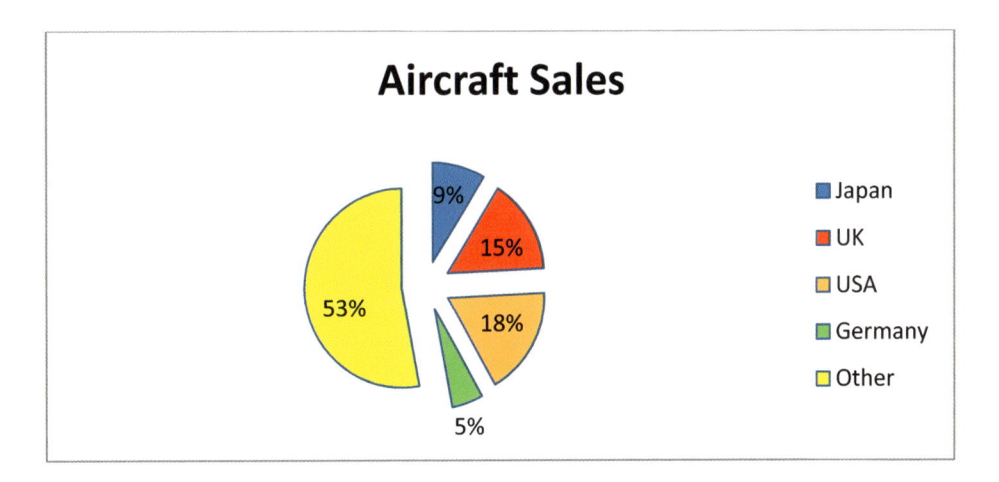

Aircraft Sales

- Japan: 9%
- UK: 15%
- USA: 18%
- Germany: 5%
- Other: 53%

A. 15,000
B. 1,750
C. 150
D. 1,000
E. 1,500

10. Using the pie chart above calculate, the combined aircraft sales for both the USA and other countries.

A. 710
B. 1,710
C. 1,900
D. 6,500
E. 7,100

11. Calculate the perimeter of the shape below.

A. 18.4 cm
B. 28.0 cm
C. 28.4 cm
D. 32.0 cm
E. 32.8 cm

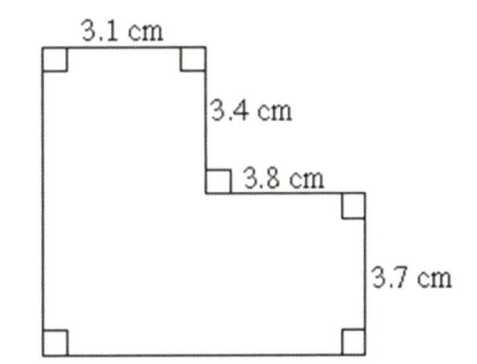

3.1 cm
3.4 cm
3.8 cm
3.7 cm

12. An office block has a length of 28 metres and width of 10 metres. What is the size of the floor space?

A. 176 m²
B. 240 m²
C. 280 m²
D. 440 m²
E. 560 m²

13. An office has a floor space of 21,000 m². If 700 people work in the office, how much m² space does each employee have?

A. 3 m²
B. 30 m²
C. 60 m²
D. 90 m²
E. 300 m²

14. New police boots cost £112; you are subsidised £42 from the force to contribute towards the boots. How much will you need to contribute?

A. £60
B. £62
C. £58
D. £74
E. £70

15. I have £13 in my wallet and spend £4.37 shopping. How much do I have left?

A. £8.73
B. £7.63
C. £8.63
D. £6.85
E. £6.53

16. How much do 24 boxes of chocolates cost at £4.10 each?

A. £98.20
B. £78.20
C. £88.40
D. £94.40
E. £98.40

17. Police in Horncastle pull over 200 suspected drink drivers over a 6 month period. There are 36 people over the drink driving limit. Out of the 200, what percentage are over the legal limit?

A. 16%
B. 18%
C. 24%
D. 30%
E. 36%

18. Each year 15,000 police officers are recruited in Scotland. 30% are female officers. How many male police officers are recruited in Scotland each year?

A. 4500
B. 7500
C. 10500
D. 12500
E. 15000

19. What is the average age of a group of children whose individual ages are 11 years, 13 years, 9 years, 9 years, and 8 years?

A. 10 years
B. 11 years
C. 12 years
D. 13 years
E. 14 years

20. How much would it cost to buy 26 jars of jam at £1.15 per jar?

A. £26.90
B. £27.60
C. £28.50
D. £29.45
E. £29.90

21. There are 635 boxes in a lorry. How many boxes would there be in 3 lorries?

A. 1,605
B. 1,805
C. 1,850
D. 1,905
E. 1,980

22. In a pick and mix you get 25 sweets in a bag for £4.00. How much does each sweet cost?

A. £0.10
B. £0.16
C. £1.00
D. £1.60
E. £1.80

23. You are trying to decide where to go on a skiing holiday. To fly to Tignes in France will take 3 hours 30 minutes; to fly to Whistler in Canada will take 6 hours 50 minutes; and to fly to Switzerland will take 4 hours 40 minutes. What is the average journey time for all three different routes?

A. 4 hours
B. 5 hours
C. 6 hours
D. 7 hours
E. 10 hours

24. PC Wood is carrying out research into the market value of narcotics. He is given four values for an eighth of an ounce of cannabis: £19, £22, £21.75, and £25.25. What is the average value for an eighth of an ounce of cannabis?

A. £17
B. £19
C. £21
D. £22
E. £24

25. Your business has yearly profits of £520,000. There are 13 equal share holders in the company. How much does each individual make in profit?

A. £20,000
B. £30,000
C. £35,000
D. £40,000
E. £42,000

PRACTICE TEST 8

12 MINS

1. At a football tournament there are 15 teams. Each team has a squad of twenty players. How many players are there in total?

   A. 200
   B. 300
   C. 400
   D. 450
   E. 500

2. The total number of hours worked by employees in a week is 390. If there are 13 employees, how many hours per work does each person work?

   A. 3 hours
   B. 20 hours
   C. 30 hours
   D. 45 hours
   E. 60 hours

3. The diagram below shows a playing field and a sand pit. Calculate the area of the playing field using the information displayed.

   A. 950 m²
   B. 1,400 m²
   C. 1,950 m²
   D. 2,400 m²
   E. 2,850 m²

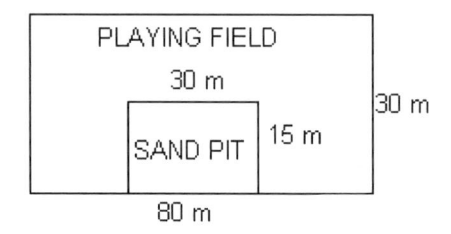

   PLAYING FIELD
   30 m
   30 m
   SAND PIT 15 m
   80 m

4. Hampshire Police operate a three-shift working pattern each day. Each shift has to have 24 police officers on duty. How many officers are required for a week's work, Monday to Friday?

   A. 36
   B. 480
   C. 420
   D. 504
   E. 360

5. Below is a scatter graph portraying sample height and shoe size for Class 4 at Edgbaston Primary School. What is the combined average shoe size for someone who is 160 cm tall and someone who is 180 cm tall?

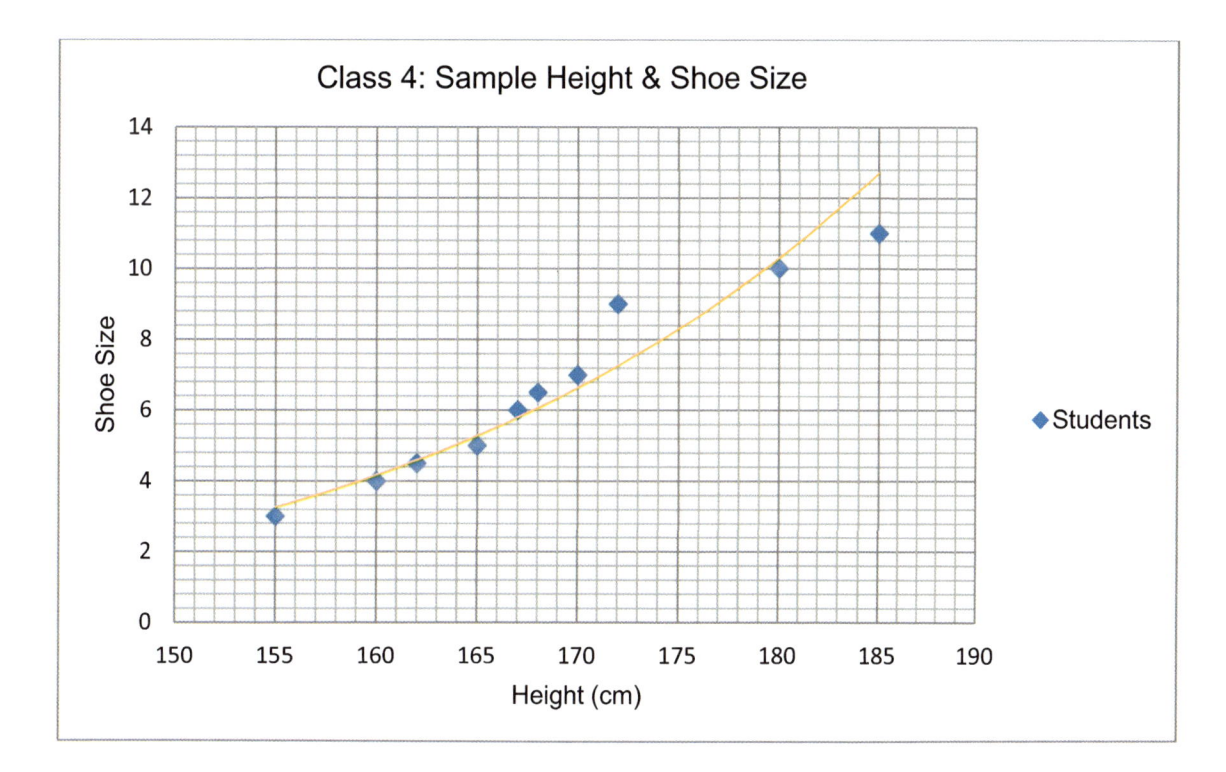

A. 6.25
B. 9
C. 7.5
D. 8.5
E. 7

6. Using the scatter graph (and trend line) above, calculate the approximate shoe size of a student who is 175 cm in height.

A. 7
B. 7.5
C. 8
D. 8.5
E. 9

7. You need to measure the perimeter of a square house. You know that one side of the house measures 15.5 metres. What is the perimeter of the house?

   A. 52 metres
   B. 62 metres
   C. 63 metres
   D. 64 metres
   E. 66 metres

8. A police officer has to put some marker cones out along a stretch of road. The road is 240 metres long and cones have to be placed 1.5 metres apart. How many cones will the police officer need?

   A. 150
   B. 160
   C. 165
   D. 170
   E. 180

9. The school run in Milton Keynes takes 3 minutes if you drive at a speed of 30 mph. How far away is the school?

   A. 1½ miles
   B. 2 miles
   C. 3 miles
   D. 5½ miles
   E. 10 miles

10. You are flying at 240 mph. How far have you travelled in 12 minutes?

    A. 24 miles
    B. 48 miles
    C. 36 miles
    D. 20 miles
    E. 40 miles

11. You have arrived at an RTA (Road Traffic Accident) and immediately call for an ambulance. The ambulance is 12 miles from your current location. You have told the ambulance that you need it here in 5 minutes. What speed must the ambulance drive at to get to the RTA on time?

A. 60 mph
B. 140 mph
C. 50 mph
D. 144 mph
E. 132 mph

12. There are 18 strawberries in a punnet. In a shop there are 12 punnets. How many strawberries are there in total?

A. 132
B. 162
C. 316
D. 432
E. 216

13. You find a purse in the street. It contains a £10 note, a £5 note, four £2 coins, three £1 coins, a 50p coin, four 2p coins and a penny. How much is there in the purse?

A. £22.59
B. £22.49
C. £24.69
D. £25.69
E. £26.59

14. A car park in Warrington issues 15 parking fines a week, each costing £60. How much does the car park make from fines every 4 weeks?

A. £1,800
B. £2,600
C. £3,600
D. £3,800
E. £4,800

15. Mary goes food shopping 3 times a week. How many times does she go food shopping in a year?

    A. 156
    B. 158
    C. 166
    D. 226
    E. 256

16. The plan below shows a layout of your garden and vegetable plot. You want to lay decking over half of the garden. What area will the decking cover?

    A. 20 m²
    B. 100 m²
    C. 125 m²
    D. 175 m²
    E. 200 m²

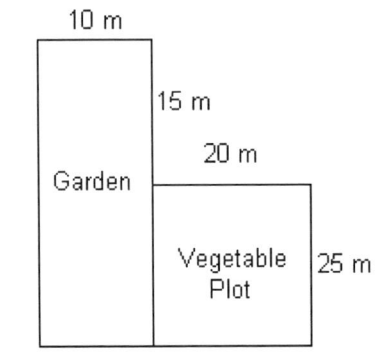

    Garden: 10 m × 15 m
    Vegetable Plot: 20 m × 25 m

17. 15% of the vegetable plot is used to grow carrots. Using the above diagram calculate what area of the vegetable plot is used to grow carrots?

    A. 25 m²
    B. 37.5 m²
    C. 48 m²
    D. 50 m²
    E. 75 m²

18. At Lowbridge High School there are 180 students taking exams. 60 of these students gain A to C grades. What is this as a fraction?

    A. 1/4
    B. 1/3
    C. 2/3
    D. 1/6
    E. 1/5

19. Your family own 5 cars. 3 of the cars are red. What is this as a percentage?

A. 30%
B. 40%
C. 60%
D. 65%
E. 70%

20. Whilst shopping I spend £1.60, £2.35, £5.60 and 74p. How much have I spent in total?

A. £10.39
B. £10.29
C. £10.49
D. £10.59
E. £11.29

21. A car ownership survey discovered that out of 10,000 cars, 2,500 were Fords. What is this as a percentage?

A. 20%
B. 25%
C. 30%
D. 35%
E. 40%

22. A motorbike is speeding at 180 mph. How far does it travel in 10 minutes?

A. 60 miles
B. 40 miles
C. 30 miles
D. 25 miles
E. 20 miles

23. A train is travelling at a speed of 80 mph. The distance between station A and station B is 200 miles. How long will it take to get from station A to station B?

A. 2 hours 15 minutes
B. 2 hours 20 minutes
C. 2 hours 35 minutes
D. 2 hours 40 minutes
E. 2 hours 30 minutes

24. You are running late for work and you have 30 minutes to get there on time. Your work is 25 miles away. What speed do you have to drive at so as not to be late?

A. 75 mph
B. 45 mph
C. 50 mph
D. 30 mph
E. 15 mph

25. What speed would you need travel at to achieve 180 miles in 20 minutes?

A. 360 mph
B. 540 mph
C. 270 mph
D. 90 mph
E. 100 mph

PRACTICE TEST 9

12 MINS

1. As a traffic officer you cover 360 miles a day. Over an 8-hour shift, what is your average speed for the day?

   A. 50 mph
   B. 60 mph
   C. 48 mph
   D. 45 mph
   E. 46 mph

2. A journey takes 2 hours and 30 minutes. You have been travelling at a speed of 70 mph. How far have you travelled?

   A. 160 miles
   B. 170 miles
   C. 175 miles
   D. 185 miles
   E. 190 miles

3. A garage is selling three used cars. The mileage on the first is 119,500; the mileage on the second is 140,500; the mileage on the third in 160,000. What is the average mileage of the three used cars?

   A. 140,000
   B. 142,000
   C. 145,000
   D. 150,000
   E. 135,000

4. At a restaurant you and your friend buy a king prawn salad (£6.95), some salmon fish cakes (£5.95), steak and chips (£11.50), chicken and chips (£10.25) and a chocolate cake (£3.95). You agree to split the bill equally. How much do you both pay?

A. £19.50
B. £19.40
C. £19.30
D. £19.20
E. £19.10

5. In a restaurant you and your friend buy a salad (£3.95), scallops (£6.95), steak and chips (£12.60), chicken and chips (£9.15) and ice cream (£1.95). You agree to split the bill equally, how much do you both pay?

A. £17.35
B. £18.40
C. £17.60
D. £15.30
E. £17.30

6. A company adds up the total number of sick days had by its employees. Out of the 52 weeks in a year it is calculated that, in total, employees have 13 weeks off sick. What is this as a percentage?

A. 25%
B. 20%
C. 15%
D. 10%
E. 5%

7. Using the diagram below, calculate the perimeter of the lily bed.

A. 70 m
B. 75 m
C. 90 m
D. 95 m
E. 100 m

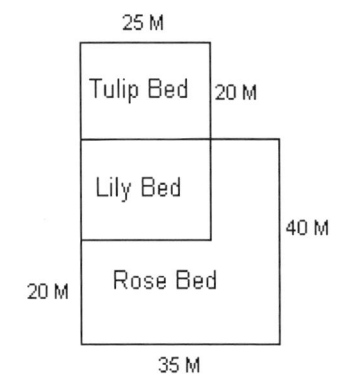

8. A bag contains 5 litres of compost soil. You calculate that 5 litres of compost will cover an area of 2.5 m². Using the above diagram calculate how many bags of soil you will need to fill the tulip bed.

A. 20 bags
B. 100 bags
C. 200 bags
D. 250 bags
E. 400 bags

9. If the police air support unit flies at a speed of 120 mph for 12 minutes, how far has it travelled?

A. 48 miles
B. 26 miles
C. 12 miles
D. 24 miles
E. 6 miles

10. A bus drives for 4 hours covering a total distance of 240 miles. What was his average speed in miles per hour?

A. 120 mph
B. 30 mph
C. 40 mph
D. 60 mph
E. 50 mph

11. Five out of one hundred police officers are injured during duty every year. What is this as a fraction?

A. 1/5
B. 1/20
C. 1/30
D. 2/50
E. 1/4

12. School dinners cost £4.75 each, and 200 children have dinners each day. How much is made from school dinners per day?

A. £550
B. £750
C. £850
D. £950
E. £1,050

13. You have a meeting at 0900hrs. You leave your house at 0840hrs. The meeting location from your house is 20 miles away. It will take you 5 minutes to walk from your car to the meeting room. What speed must you drive at to ensure you are on time?

A. 70 mph
B. 65 mph
C. 80 mph
D. 75 mph
E. 60 mph

14. Farmer Sid collects bales of hay during his autumn harvest. In his first field he collects 43, in his second field he collects 62, in his third field he collects 13 and in his fourth field he collects 42. What is the average number of hay bales he collects from his fields?

A. 39
B. 40
C. 41
D. 42
E. 37

15. There four new police recruits Mark, Laura, Ryan and Amy. Mark is 2 metres tall, Laura is 1.7 metres tall, Ryan is 1.8 metres tall, and Amy is 1.5 metres tall. What is the average height of the recruits in metres?

A. 1.77 metres
B. 1.68 metres
C. 1.62 metres
D. 1.70 metres
E. 1.75 metres

16. Below is a bar chart showing daily book sales for four stores. How many books in total does Jay's Books sell.

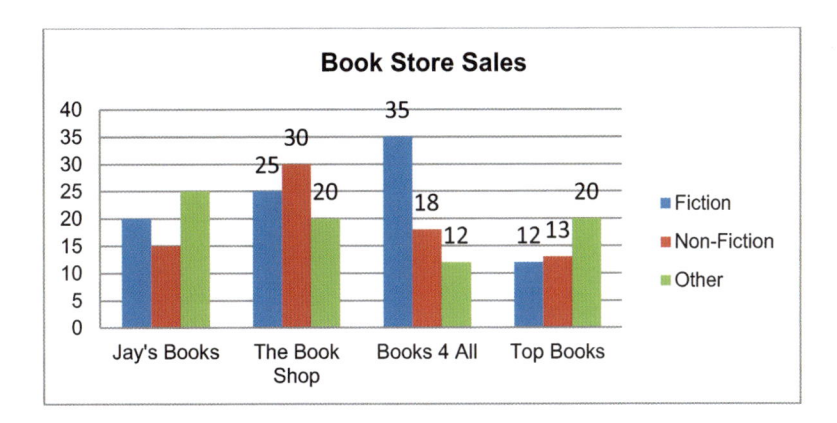

A. 40
B. 45
C. 50
D. 55
E. 60

17. What, on average, is the total amount of books sold at *The Book Shop* and *Top Books*?

A. 50
B. 55
C. 60
D. 75
E. 90

18. Whilst shopping you buy 6 items. You buy a steak costing £12.50, some vegetables costing £5.75, some cereal costing £1.21, some wine costing £10, some shampoo costing 42p and finally some sweets costing 12p. What is the average cost of the items you buy?

A. £4
B. £5
C. £6
D. £7
E. £8

19. The distance between A and B is 140 miles. It takes you 4 hours to drive the distance. What speed have you been travelling at?

A. 70 mph
B. 40 mph
C. 35 mph
D. 30 mph
E. 25 mph

20. You must arrive at work at 0900hrs. Your house is 6 miles from work. If you were to drive at 30 mph, what time would you need to leave the house to arrive at work on time?

A. 0847hrs
B. 0857hrs
C. 0848hrs
D. 0842hrs
E. 0838hrs

21. On a Saturday night the police arrest 40 people. 22 are arrested for being drunk and disorderly, 10 are arrested for assault and 8 are arrested for drink driving. What percentage have been arrested for drink driving?

A. 2%
B. 5%
C. 10%
D. 20%
E. 25%

22. During a daily patrol you average 12 miles at 3 mph. How long would it take to do a 14-mile patrol?

A. 4 hours 50 minutes
B. 4 hours 45 minutes
C. 4 hours 20 minutes
D. 4 hours 35 minutes
E. 4 hours 40 minutes

23. A train is travelling from Birmingham to Glasgow covering a distance of 390 miles. If the train's speed is 90 mph, how long does the train journey last?

A. 4 hours 20 minutes
B. 4 hours 40 minutes
C. 4 hours 10 minutes
D. 4 hours 15 minutes
E. 4 hours 30 minutes

24. You have 225 bags of sugar. If 15 bags of sugar fit in a box, how many boxes would you have in total?

A. 10
B. 12
C. 13
D. 15
E. 20

25. Whilst hiking you walk a total distance of 725 miles over a 5-day period. On average, how many miles did you walk a day?

A. 145 miles
B. 150 miles
C. 125 miles
D. 90 miles
E. 160 miles

PRACTICE TEST 10

12 MINS

1. An aircraft travels at a speed of 120 miles per hour over a total distance of 240 miles. How long does the journey take?

   A. 2 hours
   B. 4 hours
   C. 3 hours
   D. 2 hours 30 minutes
   E. 1 hour

2. How long does it take to drive 20 miles if you drive at a speed of 30 mph?

   A. 1 hour
   B. 20 minutes
   C. 40 minutes
   D. 45 minutes
   E. 50 minutes

3. A police officer walks for 15 miles in 3 hours. At what speed does the police officer walk?

   A. 45 mph
   B. 5 mph
   C. 20 mph
   D. 15 mph
   E. 10 mph

4. The distance between campsite A and campsite B is 32 miles. You walk at an average speed of 6 mph. If you set off from campsite A at 0900hrs, what time would you arrive at campsite B?

   A. 1520hrs
   B. 1410hrs
   C. 1440hrs
   D. 1610hrs
   E. 1420hrs

5. A train from Doncaster to Grimsby takes 1 hour 30 minutes. If the train is travelling at 64 mph, what is the distance travelled?

A. 94 miles
B. 96 miles
C. 95 miles
D. 92 miles
E. 98miles

6. A yacht sails at 30 mph. You are sailing across the Channel estuary which is 240 miles long. How long does it take you complete your journey?

A. 8 hours
B. 5 hours
C. 6 hours
D. 4 hours
E. 12 hours

7. You find a rucksack full of money. In the bag there is a bundle of fifty £10 notes, a bundle of twenty £5 notes and ten money bags of £2 coins, each containing 15 coins. What is the total amount in the rucksack?

A. 600
B. 750
C. 825
D. 900
E. 950

8. You annual car insurance costs £240.48. How much is this per month?

A. £20.04
B. £20.02
C. £18.04
D. £22.02
E. £22.06

9. During a week of action, the Police carry out four early morning drug raids. On Monday they enter a property at 0710hrs and leave at 0720hrs. On Tuesday they enter at 0810hrs and leave at 0840hrs; on Thursday they enter at 0850hrs and leave at 0905hrs; and on Friday they enter a property at 0700hrs and leave at 0725hrs. What was the average time spent at a property during these raids?

A. 10 minutes
B. 25 minutes
C. 20 minutes
D. 30 minutes
E. 45 minutes

10. The diagram below shows the floor plan of a house. Using the information supplied calculate the internal area of the house.

A. 880m²
B. 900 m²
C. 1,155 m²
D. 1,200 m²
E. 1,245 m²

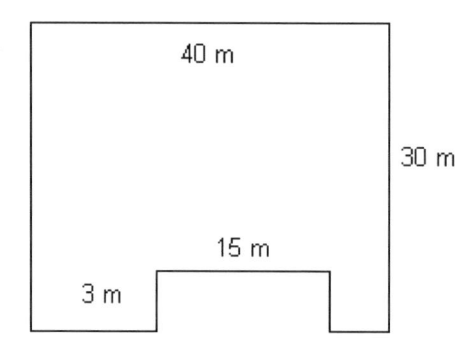

11. Using the plan above, calculate the perimeter of the house.

A. 145m
B. 146m
C. 148m
D. 152m
E. 156m

12. The train to work travels at 70 mph. The distance the train travels is 21 miles. How long does it take to travel to work?

A. 12 minutes
B. 8 minutes
C. 18 minutes
D. 15 minutes
E. 16 minutes

13. In your money box there are two £5 notes, five £2 coins, three £1 coins, six 10p coins and one penny. How much is in your money box?

A. £23.61
B. £13.61
C. £14.61
D. £16.41
E. £23.41

14. A room is 12 metres long and 5 metres wide. A carpet tile is 100cm by 100cm. How many tiles do you need to carpet the entire room?

A. 30
B. 40
C. 20
D. 6
E. 60

15. Bread costs £1.25, milk costs £2.13 and a pack of apples cost 66p. How much change will you have from £5?

A. £0.94
B. £0.96
C. £1.06
D. £1.36
E. £1.96

16. A TV has been reduced by 20% to £200. What was its original price?

A. £220
B. £240
C. £235
D. £250
E. £300

17. In Year 1 you had £200 in savings; by Year 2 this has increased to £230. By what percentage have your savings increased?

A. 10%
B. 12%
C. 15%
D. 20%
E. 25%

18. House prices have decreased by 5%. The price of your house before the decrease was £150,000. What is its price now?

A. £142,500
B. £143,000
C. £145,000
D. £146,000
E. £147,500

19. A car park has 8 floors. When completely full, each floor can hold 230 cars. How many cars in total can fit in the car park?

A. 1,440
B. 1,840
C. 2,040
D. 2,100
E. 2,140

20. A police officer works 4 day shifts per week. How many days does a police officer (without holiday entitlement) work a year?

A. 182
B. 192
C. 204
D. 206
E. 208

21. In one year, you arrest 321 people. 119 of these people are charged and the rest are cautioned. How many people are cautioned?

A. 202
B. 198
C. 200
D. 204
E. 206

22. John is 6ft 2", Ben is 5ft 9", Sarah is 5ft 4" and Garry is 5ft 7". What is the average height of the group?

A. 5ft 6"
B. 5ft 7.5"
C. 5ft 8.5"
D. 5ft 9"
E. 5ft "

23. A farmer has 5 identical fields, all of which are square fields. If one side of a field measures 500 metres long, what is the combined total perimeter of all the farmer's fields?

A. 1,000m
B. 10,000m
C. 25,000m
D. 50,000m
E. 100,000m

24. In a car park there are 1,200 cars. One sixth of the cars in the car park are blue. How many are blue?

A. 20
B. 100
C. 200
D. 250
E. 400

25. In another car park there are 120 cars. Five tenths of the cars in the car park are red. ⅔ of the red cars have five doors. How many cars have five doors?

A. 40
B. 30
C. 20
D. 70
E. 15

PRACTICE TEST ANSWERS

No	Test 1	Test 2	Test 3	Test 4	Test 5	Test 6	Test 7	Test 8	Test 9	Test 10
1	A	A	D	A	B	C	C	B	D	A
2	A	E	B	B	E	B	C	C	C	C
3	D	B	C	E	B	C	A	C	A	B
4	B	A	C	B	C	C	A	E	C	E
5	E	C	A	D	C	D	B	E	E	B
6	B	B	D	D	D	B	A	C	A	A
7	C	A	B	C	E	C	E	B	C	D
8	B	B	A	E	A	E	C	B	C	A
9	B	C	E	C	E	C	E	A	D	C
10	C	B	D	B	C	B	E	B	D	C
11	C	B	B	C	B	D	B	D	B	B
12	E	A	A	A	A	C	C	E	D	C
13	B	E	B	A	C	E	B	E	C	A
14	E	C	E	C	C	D	E	C	B	E
15	B	D	B	C	B	B	C	A	E	B
16	B	C	A	A	D	C	E	E	E	B
17	E	E	A	D	C	D	B	E	C	C
18	C	D	B	D	A	B	C	B	B	A
19	A	C	D	E	A	E	A	C	C	B
20	D	C	E	C	D	C	E	B	C	E
21	C	B	B	A	B	B	D	B	D	A
22	B	A	D	B	E	D	B	C	E	C
23	D	D	B	B	C	B	B	E	A	B
24	D	A	C	E	A	B	D	C	D	C
25	B	E	C	C	A	A	D	B	A	A

Printed in Great Britain
by Amazon